Contents

KT-439-410

Any words appearing in the text in bold, **like this**, are explained in the Glossary.

Thrills Galore

Introduction

For just over 100 years, film has surprised, delighted, shocked and angered billions of people around the world. No emotion has been spared on screen – or off it. In historical terms, 100 years is a very short time, and yet over this period film has created its own history, legend, culture and language. This book takes a brief look at one **genre** of film – the action movie, although some of the many other genres are mentioned to give a broader insight into the industry.

What makes an action movie?

From the kernel of an idea to the reviews and the **sequel**, this book charts the process of making movies for the big screen through the action movie. By looking at how one particular genre is made, it will be clear that others, such as historical epics, romances, comedies, and more, present their own challenges.

What makes a good action movie? Does it require a huge budget and a clutch of superstars? What changes in technology have made the action movie even more gripping and have enabled it to stand out among other genres? Can the storyline and the actors alone take you to hell and back in an hour and a half? We shall see that usually, it is a clever combination of all these elements.

Who makes it all happen?

Actors and directors are the shop window of movie-making. But there are countless workers behind the scenes: **set** designers, camera operators, lighting technicians, and some that you might never even have heard of – grips, **continuity** supervisors, gaffers, among many. We shall be finding out what roles they fulfil and the qualities they bring to the job. Perhaps it will attract you into the competitive world of the film industry.

What's the verdict?

Exciting examples are used throughout the book – but not as exciting as perhaps you and I might like. For the scope of the examples given here is limited to those for your age group, as judged suitable by the **censors** of the films themselves. Censorship and **certification**, reviewing and rewarding are all included in this title. So, too, are the soaring successes, the feeble flops, the characters and anecdotes that make the film world itself so irresistible – so exciting.

Going to the movies

Since the 1950s, when televisions appeared in an increasing number of homes, the film industry has had to compete with other types of entertainment. Nowadays it must try to lure audiences away from other attractions, such as computer games, the Internet and theme parks. In response to other recreational activities the film experience is becoming more and more glamorous – and technically more breathtaking than ever before. The action movie, projected on to **widescreen** and with **enveloping sound**, has taken full advantage of this. It has become one of the most popular modern genres and looks as if it will help to sustain the film industry for many years to come.

This book is to be returned on or before the last date stamped below or you will be charged a fine

1 7 APR 2023

Catherine Chambers

Heinemann
L I B R A R Y

www.heinemann.co.uk/library
Visit our website to find out more information about **Heinemann Library** books.

To order:
☎ Phone 44 (0) 1865 888066
▤ Send a fax to 44 (0) 1865 314091
▭ Visit the Heinemann Bookshop at www.heinemann.co.uk/library to browse our catalogue and order online.

First published in Great Britain by Heinemann Library, Halley Court, Jordan Hill, Oxford, OX2 8EJ,
a division of Reed Educational and Professional Publishing Ltd.
Heinemann is a registered trademark of Reed Educational and Professional Publishing Ltd.

OXFORD MELBOURNE AUCKLAND
JOHANNESBURG BLANTYRE GABORONE
IBADAN PORTSMOUTH NH (USA) CHICAGO

Designed by Paul Davies and Associates
Originated by Ambassador Litho Ltd.
Printed in Hong Kong/China

ISBN 0 431 11452 8 (hardback)　　ISBN 0 431 11457 9 (paperback)
06 05 04 03 02　　　　　　　　　　06 05 04 03 02
10 9 8 7 6 5 4 3 2 1　　　　　　　　10 9 8 7 6 5 4 3 2

British Library Cataloguing in Publication Data

Chambers, Catherine
　Film. - (Behind Media)
　1.Motion pictures - Juvenile literature
　I.Title
　791.4'3

Acknowledgements
The Publishers would like to thank the following for permission to reproduce photographs: Avid Technology Europe Ltd: p37; Big Pictures: p4; Corbis: Kevin Fleming p13, Tim Wright p32; Image Bank: p11; The James Bond Fan Club: p39; Kobal Collection: pp6, 7, 8, 12, 27, 38, 45; Media Focus: p41; Moviestore: pp15, 19, 21, 29, 40; PA Photos: p43; Pascha: p16; Rex Features: Jason Boland p23; Redferns: p34, Mick Hutson p35; Ronald Grant Archive: pp17, 20, 25, 28, 31, 44; Tony Stone: Dan Bosler p10, Laurence Monneret p9; Travel Ink: David Forman p18.

Cover photograph reproduced with permission of Moviestore Collection.

Our thanks to Steve Beckingham for his comments in the preparation of this book.

Every effort has been made to contact copyright holders of any material reproduced in this book.
Any omissions will be rectified in subsequent printings if notice is given to the Publishers.

The screaming crowds, the photographers, the television crews and the journalists are all jostling to get the best view, or even an interview, with Tom Cruise and Russell Crowe. At premières, the adoring crowds confirm that film is still hugely popular. But is stardom really so appealing? On the face of it, the glamour and the money are very attractive, but the downside is the relentless intrusion into megastars' private lives.

What is an action movie?

Ideas for films are gathered by **producers**, who are in overall charge of production and are responsible for the profit or loss made by the film. One of the first decisions that the producer has to make is which **genre** a film lends itself to. This is very important, as films follow trends. Getting the genre wrong at a particular time could be a financial disaster.

The decision makers

How an idea is filmed affects the numbers and kinds of actors and film-makers the producer employs and the cost of the movie. Action movies can be very expensive to film, and the producer has to make sure that the idea is worth the treatment. It might seem obvious which stories lend themselves to the action genre and which, say, to drama. But there can be definite choices to make. A film based on an inner-city community trying to rid its streets of drugs dealers, for instance, could be made into an action movie or a gritty social commentary – more like a drama. They could both attract a different type of audience.

Promoters, advertisers and critics probably more than anyone else have established the action movie as a genre and have broken it down into different **subgenres**. So, among others, there are action adventure movies, action sci-fi movies, spy, detective, suspense, war, comedy, spoof, ghost, disaster, historical, gangster and so on.

Ben Hur (1959), and similar types of movie were categorized as 'adventure' until the 1960s. After this time, 'action' was seen as more attractive and saleable to the public.

Keeping the edge

It seems that just about every other film genre and subgenre can be turned into an action movie depending on how it is made. But all the categorizing and advertising in the world cannot force us to find the film gripping or frightening. This is something that we each have to decide for ourselves. The task of the movie-maker is to use filming techniques, dialogue and music that provoke certain senses within us – excitement, surprise, fear, shock and at times, revulsion. Some action movies, though, hold few surprises and fall completely flat. With the huge number of films now reshown on television and video, there is little that the film-goer has not seen before. Film-makers have to become evermore inventive, which for the moment largely hinges on special effects rather than a unique storyline.

Losing the edge

The suspense and fear of some action movies is lost over time. Young people now would not consider them 'action' movies. For instance, action spy movies about the Cold War between the former communist Soviet Union and the West are less effective now among film-goers who cannot remember that political situation. The same problem can apply to World War II movies. However, the action, effects and the involvement with the characters' stories can carry the viewer through these action films without them having to fully understand the political or moral situation. *Saving Private Ryan* (1998) is a very successful example of this.

The movie-goer's taste for action has led the film industry to use evermore spectacular effects and stunts such as this dramatic escape by Tom Cruise in MI. In particular, these have enabled the action sci-fi movie to develop and become hugely popular. Films such as The Matrix *(1999 video version), with its fantastical **morphing** effects, have brought the subgenre to a new level.*

The Starting Block

What's the big idea?

Every film comes from an idea, and ideas themselves can be taken from novels, plays, short stories, poems, newspaper or magazine articles, historical episodes and characters, and modern real-life experiences. In short, just about everything, both real and imaginary!

Topicality in action movies is often successful. This means an idea is developed from a recent event, such as a war, a scandal, a crime or a political situation. Here you can see Sandra Bullock starring in The Net (1995), a good example of a modern technological and political thriller, using the theme of manipulating top secret data held on government computers.

Finding the idea

It is the **producer's** job to think of or collect ideas, and then attract finance to make the film. He or she is offered ideas by film agencies, screenwriters, directors and sometimes actors. The idea does not necessarily have to be original. For an action movie, an unusual approach, a new twist and the potential for stunts and special effects are as important as the idea itself, as the successful James Bond movies have proved.

Who owns ideas?

If a producer or a studio wants to use someone else's idea, or property, they have to pay for an option on the **rights** to use the story – in other words to put a downpayment to secure the idea. The original downpayment is about five to ten per cent of the value of full rights. It has to be renewed after an agreed period – usually a year – and then every year until the producer is ready to begin filming. At this point, another payment has to be made to firmly secure the right to film the idea. As some films take many years to get into production, options can be renewed many times, or sold to someone else if a producer cannot get financial backing to make the film (a studio usually has more financial security than an individual producer). Buying an option is like buying time – it gives the producer a chance to make a treatment from the concept and the outline (see box, page 9). The treatment is usually needed before a producer can attract financial backing, as we shall now see.

Sketching the plot

A hired writer, or maybe the person with the original idea, sketches out a brief synopsis of the story. This is known as the concept. The concept is then expanded into an outline, which again is quite short but gives more of an idea of the plot. If the outline looks encouraging and has attracted interest, the producer then selects a writer to do a treatment of it. This fleshes out the pivotal scenes, the twists and turns of the plot and the characterization, but purely as narrative with no dialogue.

An agent is negotiating an option rate for their client, who has come up with an idea that a producer is interested in. The agency will collect a percentage of the fee agreed for the idea. Agents are always on the lookout for good ideas and screenwriters.

On the job

Film agents have to be able to find good clients to represent and to pick out a good idea from the hundreds that they receive. This means that they need to know a lot about film trends and how an idea is made into a film. They also need to recognize what could be special and unique. A film agent also requires good interpersonal relationships to build up contacts among producers and directors – and keep them!

Finding the cash – fulfilling the dream

The chief job of a full **producer** is to turn an idea into a film – a dream into reality. As well as this, they have to think way beyond the making of the film to its promotion and **distribution**. The task is huge, as the producer is ultimately responsible for the smooth running of the whole project.

The world on their shoulders

The producer's responsibility includes looking after all those taking part in the film – paying them and ensuring their safety – and heavily insuring it, too, especially as the stunts in action movies can pose a great risk. The producer also has to take care that the film fulfils all legal requirements, from obtaining **copyright** for the original idea to carrying out **censors**' rulings before the film is finally released. This sometimes results in reshooting certain scenes. Most importantly, though, producers are responsible for the profit at the end of it all. This goes mainly to the investors – the people who plough money into making the film.

The big risk

Blockbuster action movies are usually financed by well-known film-making studios, or by distributors, who own the **rights** to the finished film. They make their money by selling these rights to cinema outlets and television networks wishing to screen it. Other investors include advertising agencies, banks and other financial institutions. Government arts' departments also back films. Usually, independent producers have to attract several of these investors who form a 'limited partnership', but with restrictions on the kinds of control they can exert on the producer. To attract any of these investors, the producer has sell the idea attractively – part of the publicity process, which continues throughout filming and beyond.

*Once the investors are happy with the package, they 'put together a deal' with the producer. The producer and the investors together agree the above-the-line costs, that is, known expenses before the film is shot, such as the salaries of the producer, director and stars. Once filming begins, extra money has to be set aside for below-the-line costs, such as hiring the crew and paying for the **sets**.*

Attracting the cash

Although producers working for big studios often don't need to worry about securing financial backing, an independent producer sometimes needs to gather a whole package of talent to attract the investor. The package consists of a group of film specialists and stars, and its contents vary according to the type of film being put together. In many action movies, lighting, photography and special effects are essential ingredients. The director of photography, the camera crew and effects specialists have to be well equipped to cope with the demands. A screenwriter successful in a particular **genre**, or in creating a certain atmosphere, can also be a great attraction to an investor or a buyer. But the key player in the package is usually the megastar, who is attracted by a huge salary and usually a royalty – a percentage of the takings for the film.

The production company and all the investors rely on the public to make their film a financial success. However, a lot of money is also raised through international presales. These are the rights to show the film in other countries, and are sold even before the first frame has been shot.

Actor power
The best crowd-pulling actors are usually men. For multi-million dollar feature films, especially action movies, there are few women actors who can command the same interest from investors and buyers. Jodie Foster, Sigourney Weaver, Demi Moore, Sharon Stone, Nicole Kidman, Julia Roberts, Gwyneth Paltrow and Susan Sarandon have all been recent exceptions – but there are not many more. All these women have played strong roles.

Writing it down

Once finance for the film is secured, the **producer** commissions a screenwriter to write the first draft of the **screenplay**. A full screenplay for a feature-length film will last about one and a half hours, and run to between 90 and 120 pages. This is a lot of writing, but is only the start. For it takes more than one draft to get the screenplay absolutely right.

The screenwriter for Harrison Ford, seen here with Sean Connery in Indiana Jones and the Last Crusade *(1989), might well have had to tailor the script to the star. Film stars often have some input into the final script.*

What's in a script?

As you will see when you turn the page, the draft screenplay includes not only dialogue, but also an idea of location, action and atmosphere. For the action movie, tension and explosion is often achieved through spare dialogue – keeping spoken words to a minimum – and a lot of scene-switching from one location to another. For all movie **genres**, dialogue, action and even storyline – especially the ending – can change with each draft and even during and after shooting. But the screenwriter's strong influence on the choice of location often holds firm.

Once the screenplay has been approved, the director helps the director of photography to develop a shooting script. This includes numbered shots, finer details of movement of both actors and cameras, and lighting instructions. The shooting script can take many weeks to prepare and usually does not follow exactly the original screenplay. But even this is not final. More changes are made during shooting and afterwards in **post-production** processes (see pages 36–37).

On the job

It is very hard for first-time screenwriters to get a concept and outline read by anyone in the film industry. Many ideas are developed by paid staff working for film studios, **think-tanks** of media companies, and television networks. But all of these, and independent producers, accept ideas from agents. So many writers try to get a film agent to look at their idea, remembering that they have to be prepared to write the full script if necessary. Some people start by writing for commercials, **shorts** or by writing for television soaps.

Who writes the script?

Most screenplays are collaborative. This means that different people work together – often the screenwriter, director and producer work hand-in-hand. Sometimes, there is one main screenwriter whose work is supplemented by specialists known for their ability to write certain types of scene – or dialogue for a particular type of character.

There can be some interesting choices of screenwriter. Bono, the lead singer of the rock band U2, wrote the screenplay for *The Million Dollar Hotel* (2000), starring Mel Gibson. In turn, Salman Rushdie wrote the lyrics to one of the title songs, 'The Ground Beneath Her Feet', which is performed by U2. The entertainment world is very flexible!

A young girl is asked to recite some of the script lines for a minor film role. Actors for minor roles are rarely able to alter their script. Sometimes, their dialogue and even their entire role is edited out in the post-production stage.

Inside the script

For each scene, the screenwriter has to keep the storyline moving through dialogue and action. As well as this, they have to describe the location and the behaviour of the characters. This serves as a basis for the director and other senior people to create the **sets**, choose the locations and cast the roles.

Setting the scene

As you can see from the first part of the sample script opposite, a scene can be completely dialogue-free, in which case the screenwriter has to explain the location, action and atmosphere. The director, together with the lighting director, set designer and the director of photography will then be able to work out what the scene should look like, how it should be lit, and the camera angles required. Action is related closely to location, which can set the scene for a particular type of movement, such as a car chase. Action can also be limited by the location, such as a dark, unlit house at night, although one of the most compelling features of action movies is that amazing stunts are performed in the most unlikely, often restricted places. The screenwriter's job is made even more complex if the film is to be followed by a **sequel**. It means that the writer has to think further ahead. Characters in an action movie cannot be killed off if they are needed in the sequel – buildings required for both films cannot be blown up first time around!

This sound stage, or sound-proofed film set, is where the actors will play out the script. While the screenwriter might indicate how an actor will say the words, the director will have the final say on voice quality, expression and volume.

Action instructions

For an action movie, a **screenplay's** instructions will probably include a lot of **cutting** from sets to locations and back to the set. This might involve, for example, a chase and crowds of people, which is obviously very complex to write and direct. Instructions for actions are usually written in later, according to the director's wishes. On the film script, crowd participation is marked *Crowd in* as an instruction. Action taking place in the foreground near the camera is marked *Downstage*, and action at the back of the set, away from the camera, is marked *Upstage*. If actions are critical to the understanding of the screenplay, then the screenwriter will include these on the early version.

On the job

A screenwriter has to be visual – to think pictures as well as words. They have to think time and space together – how long a certain set of actions and words should last in one place. They need to create purposeful scene-switching and to remember pace and rhythm. It is important to be subtle – to be aware what can be effectively left out, not just what can be crammed in. They have to be dramatic – to think light and dark, love and hate, vertical and horizontal, sound and silence, high and low, hot and cold, sun and snow. Their job is just to guide, though – not to do the director's job for them.

CUT TO:

20 INT. BATHROOM NIGHT

POINT-OF-VIEW SHOT (this is an eye-level shot from behind Aaron)

AARON moves slowly round the room searching for bugging devices. He breathes increasingly heavily as the search for bugs gets more futile and frenetic.

CLOSE-SHOT INTO MIRROR

Aaron feels around the mirror, looks into it and starts to scream as his fingers search all over his face and hair, his tie and his collar. He stops. Then he silently and slowly takes his contact lenses out and peers at them.

DISCOVERY SHOT TO FLOOR BY AARON'S FEET (this is a shot that moves to something not previously in view)

Aaron screams again and throws the contact lenses to the ground, crunching them.

CUT TO:

21 INT. VAN OPPOSITE AARON'S FLAT. NIGHT

BARBER is listening to Aaron's search for the bug. Can hear Aaron's scream and the crunching of the lenses through Barber's ear-pieces.

BARBER
(sneering, then laughing)

Just listen to this, Keane. Next stop the asylum!
C'mon – quickly, let's move in on him while he
can't see nothing.

CUT TO:

22 INT. BATHROOM NIGHT

Bathroom window implodes. Aaron gets flattened against bathroom wall.

This is how a film script could be laid out. The camera angle instructions and the numbering of scenes, seen here, are usually added to the final shooting script. A real script, word-processed on A4 paper, will have generous margins so that comments and alterations can be written at the side by the director and actors. The term 'CUT TO' means cutting from one scene to another. 'INT.' indicates a set interior; 'EXT.' would indicate an exterior location.

Making it Happen

The right direction

The director, usually selected by the **producer** or studio, controls the day-to-day filming of the movie. But first, he or she helps to develop the shooting script, works out where the action will take place, and much more ...

A finger in every pie

What do directors actually do? In the **pre-production** process, they influence the choice of other senior positions, such as casting director, screenwriter, director of photography, head of lighting and **set** designer. They analyse and adapt the script, guide the casting director, and work with the set designer and location manager to achieve the right background and atmosphere for the film. In the production process – the actual filming – the director guides the actors, lighting, camera and sound crew through every shot. Finally, the director is involved in the **post-production** processes, such as creating the soundtrack and **editing**. However, more film ends up on the **cutting**-room floor than many directors would like! They usually do not have total control of the finished product, as we shall see on pages 36–37.

Steven Spielberg, director and producer, is here making The Lost World: Jurassic Park *(1996). He has had some outstanding successes directing other stunt-packed action movies, such as* Jaws *(1975) and the Indiana Jones films.*

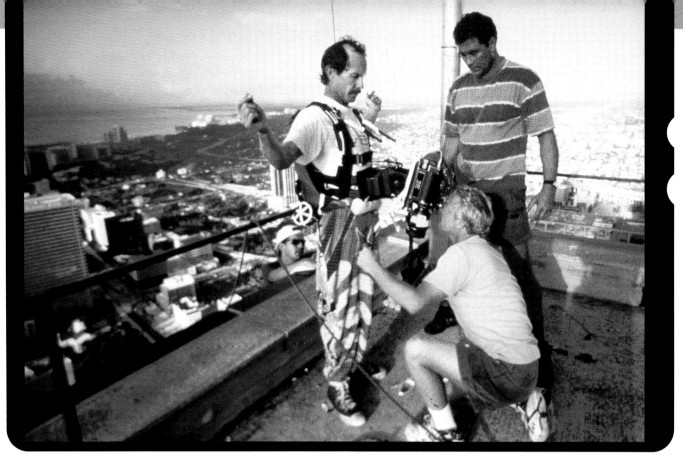

Directing stunts

In big productions, a small crew with a second-unit director is responsible for filming scenes that are not crucial to the plot, for example location, **continuity** and establishing shots (shots that set the scene). The second-unit director is also responsible for some action shots and stunts. It can often take hours to prepare a particular stunt, even if it only takes minutes to shoot. The second director works with the stunt co-ordinator, technicians, lighting and camera crew to ensure that everything will work before shooting begins. There is often no second chance to get it right, particularly on a small-budget movie. In recent years, **digital manipulation** has enabled seemingly more breathtaking and dangerous stunts to appear on screen.

One of the most difficult stunts to plan and execute is a succession of explosions, particularly if they throw things in the air and create fires. The director and the stunt co-ordinator have to make sure that automated cameras are in a safe place, that explosions occur as the cameras are running, and that the huge pistons (cannons) that shoot large burning objects into the air work properly and at the right time.

Here, a camera operator is about to jump off a building to film a sequence. When a stunt performer falls even further, from an aeroplane, for instance, a camera operator has to fall at the same time. The director will have worked out beforehand how the stunt performer will move in the sky, how close the camera operator should be at different stages, and the camera angles required. As they both fall at about 320 kilometres (200 miles) per hour, getting it right is quite a challenge.

On the job
Directors have to know everyone else's job as well as their own. They have to be able to instinctively create something natural on screen from products and processes that are totally unnatural. Some directors work their way up from the bottom, starting as the lowly gofer (you have to 'go for' – run and fetch – anything required!). But many directors study fine art or photography before attending film school, then go on to direct training films, music videos, commercials and maybe TV movies.

Location! Location! Location!

To find the perfect location, the director and location manager first study the script to understand the right kind of place and atmosphere required. Then they brief the location scout who has to find it.

The right time — the right place

One of the most important criteria for many successfully shot films is the location. The action movie is often hugely dependent on the correct choice of location, which provides an exciting or menacing environment in which the characters have to play out the action – or hide from it.

'Scouting' is the word used to describe the search for a suitable outdoor location. It is part of the **pre-production** process and can take several months, for it has to match both the screenwriter's and the director's vision of the film. It also has to be accessible to all the trucks of equipment and people required for filming. Finding the location at the right time of year is crucial – for this, too, has to conform to the script. It is no good trying to shoot a ski chase in late spring, on grass and through a thick mountain fog!

Blockbuster and cult movies have made certain locations into shrines – tourists make pilgrimages to see where their favourite movie was made. The Star Wars movies were set partly in troglodyte houses (made in caves) here in Tunisia, now a regular stopping point in the traveller's itinerary.

The space action movie Red Planet *(2000) has what one film review magazine has described as 'some suitably bleak Martian landscapes'. But where were these 'realistic' scenarios located? They could be in a rocky desert, on a shoreline or even in a gravel pit! Some planet landscapes are constructed on* **set**, *making it easier to create and control the eerie lighting effects required.*

Making it real

A location has to be easily adapted to the demands of the script. It must be possible to construct façades – outward appearances of buildings – or even whole buildings. If the film is set in the pre-motorized age, then tarmac and concrete roads have to be covered. Telegraph cables and satellite dishes must be camouflaged or removed. In short, anything that does not fit in with the setting of the film has to be avoided or obliterated. And to do this, the correct location has to coincide with co-operative local authorities and property owners. In recent years, finding appropriate buildings has been made easier by agencies that deal with properties rented out especially for filming. These range from huge country mansions, through industrial warehouses to tiny terraced cottages. Their owners know the disruption that filming causes but are able to put up with it for a generous fee!

Repairing the damage

Usually, locations disturbed by filming are restored to their normal state and facilities reinstated once the filming is over. Sometimes, though, cleaning up presents a bigger problem. Most of *The Beach* (2000) was shot on a small island off the coast of Thailand. To achieve the atmosphere of a 'typical' tropical paradise, the director ordered the clearance of a large tract of natural vegetation. Swaying palms were put in its place. But demonstrations by Thailand's ecology groups, and threats to sue the film company, forced the **producers** to spend a lot of money restoring the beach to its natural beauty.

Setting the scene

'**R**emember, a crime scene is the walls, the floor, the ceiling.' So said Denzel Washington's lead character in a 1999 movie. Exactly the same can be said of the film **set**, which the director, set designer and crew try to make perfect, right down to the last detail, and within the budget.

The importance of detail

The place, the historical period, the time of year and day and the atmosphere are the shared responsibilites of the director, the set designer and the director of photography, who helps to create the lighting. They are assisted by an authenticator, who makes sure that the decor, **props** (properties), costumes, hairstyles, and so on are correct for the nature of the film and the period in which it is set. And throughout the film, the **continuity** supervisor checks that the sets and props don't change from one sequence to the next, unless they are meant to.

Scaffolding is set up to hold the façades, buildings and other structures. With safety in mind, this and any other structure has to receive a scaff tag – proof that it has been properly inspected – before filming on or around it can take place. The catwalk is a flat base created high above a set of scaffolding to hold the lighting sytems.

Many of the advances in visual effects technology have been developed for science fiction films and natural disaster movies such as Twister (1996). The swirling wind that is blowing the actor's hair and clothes is created by huge fans.

Bank-busters

Fantasy adventure films are probably among the most difficult to create convincingly, and are often the most expensive. This, plus the problems of filming in and on water, made the futuristic fantasy *Waterworld* (1995) the most costly film ever made at the time – US$175 million. That's US$1.3 million for every minute of the finished film, which ended up making a loss at the box-office. *Titanic* (1997) has since overtaken it, costing US$200 million to complete.

How did they do that?

Action movies, particularly disaster and sci-fi ones, require scenarios that in real life would be either impossible or downright dangerous. So special effects, known as FX and SP-EFX, are used to make the impossible appear before our eyes. Some effects are mechanical – they are physical props made by special effects technicians. Mechanical effects include fake blood, so essential to many action movies. Also important to action movies are partially broken, lightweight furniture and fake glass bottles which do not do any real damage when they shatter over someone's head. Smoke is created by portable smoke machines holding gas cylinders. These are attached to funnels through which the smoke rises. The same equipment is used for making flames, the cylinders holding flammable propane gas.

Simulated floods and tidal waves are created when water is pumped through chutes attached to this dump tank, a huge water tank. As the water bursts through the chutes it merges into a wall of foaming, thrashing water.

On the job

There are many technical and practical jobs to choose from on a film set. Most need a technical qualification and experience on a smaller set. All of them need patience, as directors tend to change their minds a lot! The rigger sets up scaffolding and catwalks. Grips, supervised by the key grip, ensure that all the props are in good condition and working order. A gaffer is in charge of lighting on set and is assisted by the best boy or best girl.

Making it Real

Acting it out

A **producer** usually secures star actors before any filming begins. Supporting roles and **bit parts** are usually cast by the casting director in consultation with the director. Actors for these parts need to attend an audition during which they act pre-rehearsed pieces. They are often asked to read from the film script and are given a screen test to make sure their face looks all right on film.

In front of the camera

As a general rule, for acting in front of the camera, subtlety is often more effective than high drama. Exaggerated voice tone and texture, and dramatic body movement are unrealistic. Clint Eastwood's coach's quoted advice was, 'Don't just do something, stand there!'

How an actor reacts to a certain stimulus has to be just right for his or her role. Even in very turbulent situations, very little reaction might be in keeping with the character. Of course, as in real life, acting over-the-top is effective in the right place and at the right time. Comedy adventure is a good example, often requiring larger-than-life reaction to larger-than-life situations.

Getting into character

In spite of the differences between theatre and film acting, they do share ways of accurately portraying a part – of getting into character. Chief among these is a technique known as 'method acting'. This requires actors to get under the skin of their characters in order to feel and behave as they do. Actors often spend months studying people who in real life have roles or behaviour like the character they are to play. As well as this, they try to learn as much about themselves as possible, so that they can strip out their own personalities and instinctive reactions, replacing them with those of the character.

Action acting

The action movie requires a variety of acting techniques, depending on the film's **subgenre**. The obvious, exaggerated acting in action comedy is totally inappropriate for more serious action disaster movies, for instance. In these, visible fear is often subdued – silences and reactions are timed to perfection. The actors also have to bear in mind the action going on around them – walls of water or balls of fire perhaps – even if these are only to be **digitally manipulated** later and the actor cannot actually see them.

In action cop movies, the 'goodies' and the 'baddies' must ensure that their characters, and their relationships with each other are three-dimensional and not necessarily too obviously a contrast with each other. In the cop movie *Heat* (1995), the ruthless crime boss, played by Robert de Niro, also displays honour, loyalty and tenderness, tearing the film-goer in two with feelings of loathing and liking. This was the first film in which Robert de Niro starred with Al Pacino, who played the dedicated cop with a strange fascination for the man he wanted to put behind bars.

Making the method

Method acting techniques were developed by Konstantin Stanislavsky (1863–1938) but really blossomed in New York's 'Actors' Studio' from the late 1940s. Initially taught by Lee Strasberg, they were adopted by acting schools throughout the world. Marlon Brando was the first screen actor to apply method techniques in *The Men* (1950), in which he played a disabled World War II veteran. For this role, he spent several weeks in a physiotherapy unit studying wheelchair-users.

Many screen stars give classes in acting academies or studio workshops. Some of these are recorded on television as masterclasses that can be used more widely. One of Michael Caine's televised workshops highlighted the control, understated simplicity, timing and awareness of the camera that an actor needs to make a character work on screen.

Technical tips

In a **close-up**, the camera is a person. If the actor is talking into it, which rarely happens, then it is real. But if the actor is supposed to be talking to another person he or she can actually see, then the camera must be ignored. And yet actors must be aware that the camera will pick up everything. So if, for instance, an eyebrow is raised, then it must be for a very good reason. In many action movies, actors use controlled tightening of facial muscles to show hidden anger — an effect known as 'slow burn'.

Starlight, star bright

The stars in action movies are often well-known Hollywood actors. They might be attracted by the fee, the role, the exciting plot, unusual location, or tight, raw screenwriting. They know that an action movie is seen by a wide audience, which is helpful to their career. But while film acting seems glamorous, it involves a lot of work.

A piece of cake?

Film acting is not all money and glamour. Most stars have to work hard to get there, playing extras, walk-on parts, **bit parts** and supporting roles before stardom lifts them off the ground. Even then, filming is arduous. The bigger the star, the bigger the part with long hours of filming.

On **set**, the actor's day often begins at five or six in the morning and can end more than twelve hours later. The first stop is the make-up room, which in special circumstances may turn out to be a long stay. Film make-up is applied by make-up artists, unlike in the theatre where most actors do their own. Most roles in action movies are 'ordinary' and require no special make-up. But colour film affects natural skin tones, which has to be compensated for by applying a base over the skin. Then dark or light highlights are applied to features and cheek hollows to give shape to the face and to make sure that features show up on film.

After make-up, the actor is called by the assistant director, who holds the schedule of the day's shooting and a list of all those needed on set. There will be very little rehearsal. Film actors are expected to get to grips with the part on their own before they go on set. There, the director will rehearse and then record the scene in small bites called **takes**. One of the most important parts of the rehearsal is blocking. This means showing actors where they should stand and move, and the camera crew where they should be filming from. Once the director is satisfied with a particular filmed sequence, an actor might not be needed for several hours before their next one. Waiting is one of the most difficult and boring tasks for the film actor.

Tinseltown

While the Hollywood legend is not quite what it used to be, it still attracts young, hopeful actors in their droves. It was here in Los Angeles that the great studios – MGM, Paramount, Universal, among others – dominated film production and created the formula- and **genre**-based movies, of which action has proved to be one of the most successful. These kinds of studio once held lead actors to long contracts, but today actors are more independent. Their agents send them scripts from studios and **producers**, and advise them on the roles to accept. Many actors rely on their agent to mould their career, helping them to choose the right step up through the ranks to stardom. A trade union, the American Screen Actors' Guild, secures minimum rates of pay.

Mel Gibson

Mel Gibson has starred in some of the most popular and unusual action movies. He gained his first international role as the hero in the futuristic action movie *Mad Max* (1979) because the Australian director, George Miller, decided that Gibson looked 'wrecked enough' for it. He has played a similarly crazy character in the Lethal Weapon cop action movies.

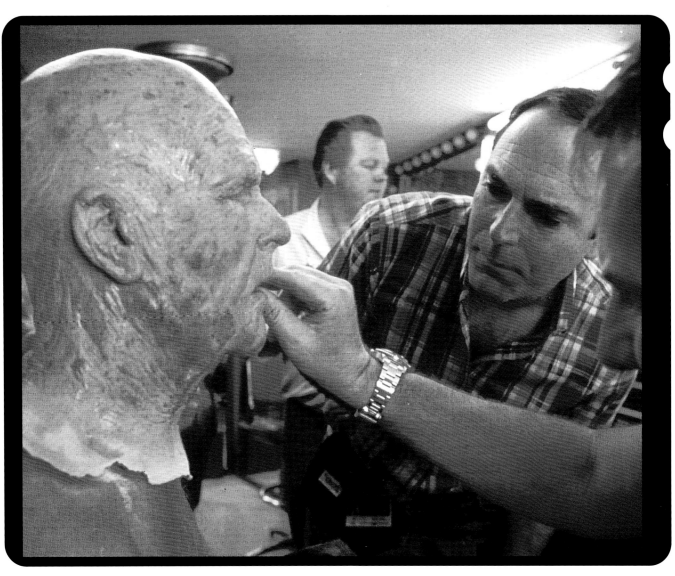

*This transformation is being achieved using prosthetics – shaped pieces of latex or plastic stuck on to the face with adhesives and blended in with make-up. Today, transformations are made seamless on screen by **digital morphing**. Make-up artists are now rewarded for their creative work with Oscars – the first given in 1981 for the spooky (and funny!) werewolf transformations in* An American Werewolf in London.

Acting for all?

Most action movie stars are white males, and it has taken a long time for women and black actors to break into the genre in other than support roles or roles that stereotype them. The action cop movie *Shaft* (1971) was a landmark production, in that it was a mainstream movie starring an African-American actor, Richard Roundtree, and featuring several others. Roles for black actors have become more plentiful and varied since the US director, Spike Lee, came on the scene.

All under control?

The director first has to work out how every shot will look and how a sequence of shots will be put together. For action sequences this can involve the assistance of the stunts co-ordinator. But the director also has to imagine and plan the special effects that will be created after filming and during the **editing** stage.

Time is money

The role of the director is to use the technology and art of film photography to tell the story, characterization and emotion of the **screenplay** using a combination of science and senses. In working out the scenes and the shots, the director also has to be aware of time and budget – the one greatly affecting the other. But the director is never sure exactly how many **takes** each shot will require, and therefore how much cost will be incurred.

An action movie with a lot of stunts can take longer than, for example, a historical drama. Normally, though, a day's filming will create two to three minutes of finished film, which means that a full-length feature movie will take about two months, or longer, to shoot. To save time and money, all the scenes that need to be set on one location are planned and shot in one go, maybe over a week, even if they do not follow the order of the screenplay. This means that the unit **continuity** supervisor has to keep an eye on the **props** and costumes. For example, about three-quarters of the way through an action movie, a character sustains a broken arm during a fall. This scene has to be shot with others that occur in the same location but at the beginning of the movie. When the film crew moves to a different location to shoot scenes at the end of the film, the unit continuity supervisor has to make sure that the actor with the 'broken arm' is still wearing a plaster cast.

Planning the stunts

Action movies need very careful planning, possibly more than any other **genre**. The mechanics of stunts are worked out separately while the director has each action shot sketched on detailed storyboards. Simpler scenes need only continuity sketches, in other words, an idea of what action is taking place in a particular sequence of shots. The director shows the stunt co-ordinator the aim of each sequence, the effects that he or she needs, and the location in which the stunt is to take place. Then, within a budget, the stunts co-ordinator prepares the stunt with the help of technicians, engineers, explosives and safety advisers, as well as experts in certain techniques such as parachuting, white-water rafting, or similar skills. Specially-made vehicles, such as cars with safety roll-cages built inside, must be checked. If a stunt needs to be photographed from overhead, in, for example, a helicopter or hot-air balloon, then these have to be hired and their operators briefed. The location has to be assessed by the director of photography to make sure that they can site and move cameras effectively. Stuntmen and women need to be well rehearsed and be wearing the correct protective clothing, such as fireproof garments in a car stunt. Dummies have to be constructed and dressed.

Preparation is the key to success. It can take a day's work just to prepare a sequence that lasts only a few seconds on screen. But stunts are so expensive to produce that it is important to get them right first-time round. The walk-through rehearsal before shooting begins is only a guide for the cameras, sound and lighting. It will not include the stunt itself if the equipment used is at risk of being damaged.

On the job

Stunts co-ordinators need to be good at sciences and technical subjects to enable them to create everything from falling heroes to walls of fire. They require the imagination and practical skills to turn drawings and descriptions into reality. However, their overriding concern must be the safety of all the crew, actors and stunt personnel. Good organizational skills are essential because stunts have to work on time – and first time!

Storyboards created for complex action scenes are detailed, shot-by-shot illustrations showing the movement and positions of the actors and props, dialogue and any music or sound effects required. The production designer, crew and actors can see clearly the aim of each shot and what they will be required to do for each one.

The tools of the trade

A movie camera captures a rapid succession of still images on a light-sensitive film. The quality and strength of the light source, together with the type of camera film used, affects the shades and tones of the film, the shadows, and therefore the mood. But the director of photography also needs to angle the lighting and move the cameras in certain ways in order to create the right effect.

Moving the movie camera

The director of photography uses cameras and lighting together to capture the action and atmosphere of each shot. But rapid movement in action sequences, and changing light makes it especially difficult to direct and control these sequences. An example of this is a night-time scene with lots of explosions.

*The Steadicam, a **hydraulic brace** which holds the camera on to the operator, enables movement without shaking the image. This is especially useful for action shots. Hand-held cameras are now used a lot for disjointed, frantic action shots.*

The movie camera has to be very mobile. It must be able to move horizontally around on its axis while at the same time having the facility to tilt up and down. This is often used to represent eye movement realistically as a character looks across the landscape or up at a window. It is one of the **point-of-view techniques** that makes you understand what the character sees and feels, maybe in the tense moments before action takes place, or during an action sequence itself.

There are many different camera lenses and angles used to make movement exciting. The zoom lens enables the camera operator to 'move' close to the action, then draw away from it, without transporting the camera or losing the subject.

Technical tips

Action sequences viewed from a greater distance — maybe a medium shot, for instance — often require the camera to move with its operator on a stand. This is set on wheels, called a dolly, or a crab dolly, which is constructed to swivel in all directions, or a velocitator dolly, which is a camera mounted on a crane for overhead shots. These vehicles can run along tracks to help them keep up with the action.

Light and shade

Lighting intensity, colour and contrast has to suit the kind of camera and film that the director of photography has chosen to provide shape, light and shade to the sequence being shot. He or she uses different types and strengths of lamp and shades of **filter** to achieve this, as well as angling the lamps so that they create the right shadows – or no shadows at all.

General lighting illuminates a wide area, while specific lighting has to be positioned to highlight a particular subject – and action movies are mostly about people rather than empty spaces! In an average daytime sequence on **set**, where the director needs little tension or atmosphere, a room needs a **diffused fill light** that fades the shadows, while the subject requires a back light to outline it and a key light to give it body and make it stand out.

Shooting a daytime action chase sequence outside, with the actor running at a diagonal towards the camera, the director of photography might choose natural sunlight as the general lighting, which will allow a shadow to be cast. Then he or she may focus specific lighting on the actor, perhaps angling high-powered lamps on to the actor's body. Lamps can be hard and direct or soft and diffused, and can be varied in shade or tone by filters. These are clipped over the camera lens to absorb certain frequencies of light and allow others to shine through.

This helicopter is being used to film action inside and around it without actually taking off. But helicopters are also used to film sequences from a height. These are particularly effective if actors or vehicles are moving diagonally across the screen from one corner to the other. This is known as diagonal action.

Lights, camera, action!

The assistant director holds the timetable, or schedule, of each day's shooting on call sheets. He or she organizes the production crew, while the **unit production manager** makes sure that the equipment gets to the **set** or location on time. Everything is geared to a successful day's shooting so that the schedule is met.

On your marks

Shooting can start very early, especially on an indoor set which might need **prop** changes if different scenes of the film are being shot the same day. On an outside location, shooting depends a lot on the light that the scene requires and the amount of equipment that needs to be set up. For an action movie such as *The Perfect Storm* (2000), this can include making sure that the dump tank (see page 21) and the rollers that work the wave-making machines are operating properly. Stunts must be carefully checked to make sure that everything will work in the correct sequence and all the safety precautions are in place.

Lighting is placed according to the **lighting plot**, and the assistant camera operator checks that the right **filters** or shades are attached. They make sure that the output, or intensity, of each lamp is consistent with the instructions in the lighting plot. The assistant camera operator fits the camera with the film cartridge. The camera is then positioned, ready for the first **take**. The **boom operator** ensures that the microphones will reach the actors while the assistant sound recordist fits the recording tape and checks sound levels. Meanwhile, the actors are being dressed and made up, either in rooms on set or in trailers on location.

Get set

The assistant director calls the actors. A walk-through or dry run with the actor or the stand-in actor checks that lighting and camera positions are correct. Then the director might settle down in the director's chair, waiting to view the first take on a small monitor in front of him or her. This is connected to a tiny video camera attached to the **optical viewfinder** on the camera, through which the camera operator sees the frame which he or she is shooting. The monitor enables the director to see what the camera operator sees, although the camera operator is the expert who will determine the final quality of the film.

Go!

Outside a set, a red light is switched on to tell people that the shoot is about to begin and that no one must enter. Whether inside or outside, the camera operator calls out 'Speed!', which means that both the camera and the sound equipment are synchronized and running. The **clapperboard**, with the number of the shot and take, and the date and time of day on it, is snapped shut or, if automated, makes an electronic noise. Shooting begins.

While the film is being shot, the camera crew keep a shooting log, or diary, in which the cameras, filters and film used for each shot are taken down, plus any shots that the film crew believe are no good. The assistant director also takes notes on the day's shooting. The assistant producer tries to make sure that the production goes to plan and that nothing extra will be needed – nothing to ruin the budget!

Making sure

The director often orders cover shots of everything – a second shot of the same thing, just in case the film footage cannnot be used for some reason. When the footage is complete, or 'in the can', the unit is able to wrap up for the day. The runner races off with the film to the processor, which is then sent to the editor for choosing the best takes. That evening the director and other members of the crew and actors sit down and examine the **rushes** – the result of a hard day's work.

At the end of the day the unit crew can pack up their equipment and go 'home'. The same set, though, might be needed for the following day but with different props. This might be because the next sequence of shots occurs much later on in the film and so will need to look different. Whatever the reason, it means that the set has to be re-dressed by the set dressers.

Putting it Together

Sounds good

A movie soundtrack has to be clear but it must also be meaningful as it can add so much to the understanding and atmosphere of a film. On **set** or location the sound is recorded separately from the visual film by an audio recording machine on a quarter-inch magnetic track or r-dat **digital** cassette.

Sight and sound

At the beginning of a **take** the sound recordist loads the tape recorder and checks sound levels, while the **boom operator** makes sure that the microphone is positioned effectively. We saw on page 30 that at the start of a take, a **clapperboard** marks the moment at which sound recording and filming begin for each take. Interlocking synchronization equipment in the film and sound machines ensures that filming and sound recording begin at the same time. Some equipment now uses a digital time-code method of synchronization. Synchronization is vital at the **editing** stage when the images and sound are matched up.

Once filming begins, the sound recording equipment picks up dialogue and background sounds, whether natural or created on set or location, through microphones held at the correct angle above the action. Some are attached to fixed arms called booms, while others are mounted on hand-held ones called fishpoles.

Sounds natural

It is easy to think that everything we hear on film was going on as it was being shot. But nothing could be further from the truth! In the **post-production** editing stage, the sound editor has to remove any unwanted background noises. Actors have to re-record any dialogue that is unclear and match their voice to the lip movements on screen. In a disaster action movie such as *Twister* or *The Perfect Storm*, speech has to be heard over the crashing of flying debris or the loud sloshings of water.

Sounds special

Some special sound effects have to be created in the studio by the foley artist, named after Jack Foley who was the famous special effects artist at Universal Studios in the 1930s. Other special effects are bought in from sound archives or, more recently, loaded down from mixing **consoles**, where they are held in their hundreds. Library or stock shots that are added to the film often have unsuitable soundtracks or are mute – they have no soundtrack – so one has to be created.

Action sequences often need a medley of soundtracks holding different sound effects, especially during a chase sequence with, for example, the sound of car engines, screeching tyres and changing background noises as the chase moves through different scenarios. All these separate tracks, plus the music track, are checked so that their sound outputs are at the right levels, then mixed together by the sound mixer. This is usually dubbed on to a magnetic stripe on the edge of the show print, which is screened in the cinema. Here, the electric signals held on the magnetic stripe are translated back into sound by the film-projecting equipment.

On the job

Sound effects specialists need to be aware of the subtleties of sound qualities, pitch and volume. They have to be very imaginative to feel what a particular sequence requires to make it sound real, or even out of this world. Effects specialists must be creative, too, knowing what will make the different sounds needed and being able to reproduce them. They need good technical sound recording skills.

*In the early 1960s, a portable high-quality recording machine called a Nagra hit the film world. Together with the new, quieter, lightweight Eclair 16mm camera it revolutionized independent film-making. A rush of **arthouse** and horror movies was proof that film-making could be small-scale and cheap.*

Making music

The music score is composed and compiled once the film has been **edited**. In most films, the score is a combination of original music composed especially for the film, pre-released or canned music, and sometimes source music played on screen by, say, a CD player or a 'live' pop group.

Good arrangements

Music fulfils several roles in a film. Both the title track and recurring theme tune help to give the film an identity and create a particular mood. After other sounds, or even silence, a theme tune can mark a starting-up point for action – it can help to move the film along. Subtle variations – maybe a different instrument or a change in tempo (speed) – can alter the mood of a particular scene.

An orchestra plays the music for a film score inside a very large soundproofed room called a scoring stage. Behind them there is often a screen on which the film is projected. The conductor stands in front of the film and uses it, along with the score and cue cards, to help him or her pace the music.

A film's main characters often have their own separate theme tunes, which help us to recall their role in the film or alert us to their re-entry on to the scene. However, music is not supposed to be the star – rather a subtle hook for us to pull together the strands of the plot, the characters and the overall idea of the film. For much of the time it serves as a background, enhancing the emotions within the audience.

Some composers are famous for providing music for a certain type of film, while others have adapted their skills to a wide variety of **genres**. The pulsating, foreboding rhythms in the disaster action movie *Jaws* (1975), the swashbuckling score of the Indiana Jones blockbusters, the musical magnificence of the space epic *Star Wars* (1977) and the eerie melodies of *Schindler's List* (1993) were all the work of one composer – John Williams.

The power of music

Arranging effective music has become yet another highly-skilled and specialized job. Formula Bond movies have formula title tracks and formula music scores. Their age-old theme tune is freshened and rearranged with each movie. Just a few bars of it are inserted here and there to remind us that we are watching Bond, the legend. Occasionally, though, it is used just to help continuity between sequences. Bond theme tunes are now regularly performed, and sometimes written, by famous pop stars or groups. The theme tune for *The World is Not Enough* (1999), was performed by Garbage. Various other artists have included Paul McCartney and Shirley Bassey.

Here, Bryan Adams is singing the number-one hit theme tune to Robin Hood – Prince of Thieves *(1991). When title music such as this is released as a single, it often tops the charts on both sides of the Atlantic. Both the record and the pop video are certain money-makers and perfect advertisements for the film itself.*

On the job

A film-score composer understands how different musical instruments, including **synthesized** sound, can be used individually and together to good effect. He or she reads and writes **musical notation** fluently. More than this, the composer matches music to motion and emotion. Most composers study music composition at college and write music for other media besides film, such as TV commercials.

35

Wielding the knife

One of the most important parts of film-making is **editing**. This is the skill of choosing the best **takes** of shots, and the right lengths of sequences, and then piecing them together slickly to deliver the plot and create the right atmosphere for the film.

The cutting-room floor

Editing begins after the first day's shooting when the **rushes**, sometimes known as 'dailies', are viewed by the director, the director of photography and other members of the team. At this stage, obvious mistakes are discarded and the best takes of each scene are kept. If none of the takes are good enough, then they have to be reshot.

When filming has been completed, the editor's first job is to synchronize the sound to the images by matching up the beginning of each shot with the sound of the **clapperboard**. Then the scenes, still in the wrong order, are assembled into their correct order on film by **cutting** and splicing ('sticking' together again). The end result is known as the rough cut. After this, the editor's hard cutting work really begins. Using techniques such as dissolving and fading, which merge shots into each other, the scenes are artistically put together. The final result is the slick fine cut. A copy of the fine cut, known as the work print, is then viewed by the director and **producer**.

All change

Once the director and producer have passed the work print, the film is matched with the edited soundtrack. Special optical effects, titles and credits are then added. This answer print (also known as the approval print) is still vulnerable to last-minute changes. It is the first time that a complete colour-and-sound print has been seen, and sometimes it has to be sent back to the laboratory for colour grading or other tweaks. At this stage the movie is often tested on an audience and the **censors** before the original negative, incorporating any final changes, is made. The final alterations are made by the producer. These are not always approved of by the director! Nevertheless, this **final print** is sent for copies to be made and distributed.

Getting it right

A good editor cannot afford to be sentimental, and many hours of hard work end up on the cutting-room floor. But this is often especially beneficial for the action movie, which can rely on quick glimpses of a character or location, snatched conversations, and flashes of action in the dark to heighten the tension.

Editing styles have changed over the years, just as have directing and acting styles. The action movie has used many fashions to good effect. These include documentary-style filming techniques which use hand-held cameras, and rough, punchy editing, involving techniques such as jump-cutting and cross-cutting.

Jump-cutting involves removing sections of a shot such as a long, tracking shot and splicing the pieces together again, achieving a jerking, edgy effect. Cross-cutting moves back and forth from completely different shots, often showing a reaction of one character to the actions of others. In recent years, **morphing** has become an important feature of many action movies. This **post-production** effect is the **digital manipulation** of images to make solid objects appear to change, transforming reality into animation and back again.

Editing can now be done digitally. This AVID editing software enables the editor to make choices and changes on screen by digitally cutting takes and moving around sections of scenes. The editor can run several takes of a particular scene on the screen at the same time, enabling them to cut the best bits from each take and put them all together. This process is rather like cutting and pasting text on a computer screen using a keyboard. Digital editing allows for greater control and precision. It's also a 'loss less' environment, meaning that there is no loss of film quality and no introduction of noise and hiss on the soundtrack.

Happy endings

In big American studios in particular, it is often not acceptable to have a negative or unresolved ending to a movie – unless, like *Bonny and Clyde* (1967), there is a real-life one that cannot be fudged. So a director's unhappy or vague ending is often cut and something positive and definite is substituted. It is believed that this 'happy factor' will keep attracting audiences to the cinema. But when a film is re-released or released on video, the director sometimes gets the chance to use the original ending, or other scenes that were cut by the producer. This version is then known as the 'director's cut'.

What do they think of it?

Once the **final print** has been made the director has nothing more to do and bows out. But then the publicity and promotion machine starts rolling in earnest and the **censors** begin to play their part in the success or failure of the movie.

Testing, testing

Before the very final changes have been made, the film is tested on a selected audience and is shown to the press. Stills and trailers are selected for promotional material and the long-planned advertising campaign now has strong visual images to attract interest. But what the **producer** is really waiting for is the 'ticket' – the censor's **rating**. This can seriously alter the public image of the film and can wipe out a large amount of money at the box office by excluding certain age groups. Later, ratings can affect the screening hour on television. A video version, though, can be re-**edited** to make it suitable for a younger audience. For instance, you will probably not be able to see *The Matrix* in the cinema, but the video version has been edited so that you can watch it in your own home.

It seems unbelievable that our cute friends Kermit and Co. could be the subjects of censorship in the first Muppet movie. But in 1979 the New Zealand film board cut it on the grounds of unnecessary violence. In the late 1990s, and following on especially from works by directors such as Quentin Tarantino, Hollywood stars in particular have voiced their unease at the increasing intensity of violence on screen.

Posters, hoardings, interviews with the stars, and tantalizing trails of action sequences for TV film review programmes and commercials were all used to advertise this Bond movie. Pokémon: The Movie (2000) was promoted by its own pre-movie products. Japanese fans alone spent about £2.5 billion (US$4 billion) on these in the first eighteen months.

What shall we call it?

Titling can happen at the last minute. Choosing different titles for separate markets is quite common, reflecting different tastes and hopefully drawing in maximum audiences on all sides of the world. Often, the two titles seem totally unconnected – a 1949 thriller about a sinister stranger trying to steal a politician's soul was called *Alias Nick Beal* in the USA and *The Contact Man* in the UK. More logically, *Wall Street* (1987), a movie about crime in the financial world, was initially called *Greed*. *The Return of the Jedi* also started with a different name – *The Revenge of the Jedi.*

Time to Let Go

Seen on screen

Once the movie has been made, it goes to the **distributing** company, which makes copies of the film and distributes them to cinema outlets. The distributor also organizes marketing, advertising, merchandising and all media interviews of the director and the stars involved in the production.

The digitally-animated action adventure Toy Story 2 *(2000) took around £8 million in box-office receipts during its first week in the UK, and attracted a wide age group.*

Who makes the money?

Major distributors take a huge fee from cinemas for the first week of showing – sometimes 90 per cent of the takings. When you consider that the action disaster movie *The Perfect Storm* (2000) made over $4 million in the USA in its opening weekend alone, you can see why they do this!

Pictures to the people

☆ A circuit release is when a film is distributed to a circuit – a large number of cinemas owned by one company. The biggest American circuit is the United Artists' Theater Circuit which owns about 1700 cinema screens.

☆ A floating release is when a film is distributed to all cinemas wishing to show it.

☆ Four-walling is when a distributing company pays an exhibitor an agreed price to use their theatre. The distributor sees to all the promotional work, fixes the ticket price – and then pockets the profits from the takings.

☆ Renters are cinemas or individuals who get **rights** to exhibit a film for a length of time agreed with the distributor. For this, the distributor receives either a set fee, a percentage of the receipts, or both.

The cinema experience

Modern multiplex and megaplex cinemas, with their thick carpeting, snack bars and games rooms take us back to the early idea of cinema as a luxurious night out. The film industry is faced with huge competition from television, computer games and the Internet. It has responded not only with gimmicks and facilities but also by giving people a wide choice of films within one building. This choice extends to format and sound. In 1953, the success of Cinemascope, with its **widescreen** format, proved that films could prise some people away from their television sets. Over the last few years, the IMAX system, with its six-soundtrack film and surround picture, has tried to do the same. Action and space fantasy **genres** have, in the use of dynamic effects, made the most of this development. In the same way, blockbuster action movies have taken advantage of the recent creation of **enveloping sound**. The viewer really feels that they are part of the action. Action-responsive seats, which move with the motion on screen, and 3-D vision using special glasses have also made the action movie experience excitingly real.

Since its development in 1974, this platter projector, also known as the 'cakestand', has superceded the upright projector. Its advantage is that the film does not need to be rewound.

Technical tips

Projecting a movie on to the screen reverses the processes that put it on to film. In other words, instead of a light source projecting images through a lens on to a negative film, a projector focuses an incredibly strong xenon light through positive film and a lens magnifies and focuses it on to a screen. Recent developments in **digital** technology mean that very soon the whirring of the film projector could be a thing of the past. In 1999 there was the first all-digital showing of the action sci-fi *Star Wars Episode 1: The Phantom Menace.*

The verdict and the future

After the film **preview** the **producer**, director, actors and crew wait anxiously for the critics' verdicts. Poor reviews affect not only the box-office takings but also their own reputations. But the final and most important verdict comes during the first week of the movie's release, when the public either flocks to it or rejects it.

Striking gold

Cynics say that a box-office hit depends on a star, a script, marketing and merchandising – but especially the star. However, in 1999 the president of Paramount Studios, Sherry Lansing, reassured the film-going public that a good script and a good story are the keys to the treasure chest. It helps if film critics are on your side, though, for their initial reaction can ruin the chances of a film and all those who worked on it.

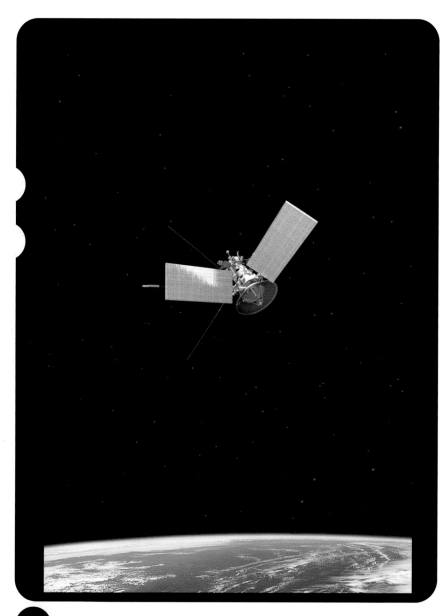

The critics

Pauline Kael, one of the most feared and respected US film critics ever, penned her reviews for *The New Yorker* from 1968 until 1991, when she went into semi-retirement. Some of her comments went against popular opinion, but her shrewd remarks often pinpointed the kinds of things that most of us find difficult to express. That is what good critics do. Sadly, she often slated action movies such as *The Return of the Jedi* (1983) which she called a 'junky piece of moviemaking', and *Airport 1975* (1974) – 'processed schlock'! Kael's biting style is not used by all film critics. The UK's well-known Jonathan Ross and the growing number of young TV film reviewers prefer a lighter, more humorous tone.

*But what of the future of the big screen itself? We saw on page 41 that 1999 witnessed the first projection of a **digital** film copy. The next step is almost certainly to beam film into the theatre via satellite.*

Winning ways

Oscars, Golden Globes and European film awards are the shop window for the film world, where producers and directors watch out for the next rising star. The awards' season begins in late January with the Golden Globes, which are good indicators for the nominees and final winners of the Academy Awards (Oscars) in March or April.

Some awards are handed out at film festivals such as Cannes and Vienna. Here, little-known film-makers and cult movie-makers are given a chance to show what they can do. One of the most coveted awards is the Palme d'Or given to the best film shown at Cannes. The American MTV Awards, though, probably give the public more of an idea of the work involved in action movies than any other award, as they include categories such as the best fight and the best villain.

Arnold Schwarzenegger and his wife, Maria Shriver, arrive at the Annual Academy Awards. Action movies regularly win Oscars, particularly in the special effects and photography categories. But while they are often nominated for 'Best Picture' and 'Best Director' awards, these often go to a more 'serious' type of film.

Success in the future?

The quirkiness of Australia's Mad Max futuristic action movies and the grit and rawness of Britain's tense *Trainspotting* (1996) are just two examples of successful movies outside Hollywood. These individual successes have been hailed as the 'new dawn' in these nations' film industries and have led to a cry for more internal **investment** to put them on a par with Hollywood. It is doubtful that this would happen – and is it desirable? These countries' film-makers are very individualistic, yet collectively they give their nations' film industries a distinctive style. It is perhaps best to leave huge blockbusters, especially expensive action movies, to Hollywood, where they do them so well.

Magic action moments

What does an action movie leave us with? What will we remember of it years later? Will we remember it at all? What will its star **rating** be when it reaches the small screen? Time will tell, and often it takes many years for a film's classic qualities to be fully recognized. But whatever the final verdict, the action movie often provides some of the best moments on film.

Unforgettable

Three Mini-Coopers are skidding periously close to the water in The Italian Job's *(1969) famous car-chase sequence.*

According to continuous research polls, it has been found that more than all the heart-stopping action and the spectacular effects that directors throw at us, it is human emotion, relationships and words that remain uppermost in the minds of film-goers. Having said that, who can forget memorable sequences of car races and ski chases? Everyone has their favourite movie moments. Here are just a few that have been quoted as exciting, memorable, dramatic, and so on.

- In *The Italian Job* (1969) a gang steals $4,500,000, sabotages the city's computerized traffic control system, and then drives dangerously fast around the narrow, blocked streets of Turin in Italy. Amazing stunts in three tiny Mini-Cooper cars confirmed this movie as an action classic.

- There are so many Indiana Jones moments to choose from – spectacular explosion sequences springing immediately to mind. But for sheer thrill, what about Harrison Ford and Kate Capshaw's long journey at breakneck speed down a mine shaft in a rail car in *The Temple of Doom* (1984)?

- That Bond ski-parachute chase – the one in *The Spy Who Loved Me* (1977) – took £250,000 from the budget and was shot in one go. The part where the falling ski hits the opening parachute as Bond tries to float down to safety was actually an accident, but makes the sequence even more breathtaking. In reality, the stunt artist was putting his life on the line.

- In another Bond film, *The World is Not Enough* (1999), the seemingly indestructible MI6 building explodes and Bond shoots out into the Thames in a speedboat – the beginning of an impossible but thrilling chase around the waterways of London.

- With chases in mind, the action cop movie *Bullitt* (1968) cannot be left out. Its dizzying roller-coaster route up, down and round the streets of San Francisco is like a theme-park ride.

- What about action-packed fights? *Charlie's Angels* (2000) is one of the few you will find featuring women. In order to create these slick manoeuvres, Drew Barrymore and Cameron Diaz had to be coached eight hours a day for three months, and Lucy Liu for two. Filmed on closed **sets**, these breathtaking sequences were a well-kept secret.

- Some films leave us with lasting legacies in our language. The way, or the place in which something is said, make it memorable. The catchphrase, 'I'll be back' was immortalized by Arnold Schwarzenegger in the Terminator films (1984 and 1991).

- And now for some special effects – *The Matrix* (video 1999) provides some superb **morphing** sequences when the hero, Neo, touches a mirror which transforms into liquid mercury and envelops him, transporting him from the dream world into the real one.

The spectacular effects and gruesome action of the dinosaurs in Jurassic Park (1993) made this movie one of the all-time greatest box-office hits, grossing more than $1 billion.

Glossary

arthouse   movies that are not mainstream, but are often interesting ideas or directed in an unusual way; they are usually made on a tight budget and make very little money

bit part   minor role in a movie

boom operator   operator of a telescopic arm that holds a microphone over the heads of actors

censor   someone who decides that a film or part of a film contains too much violence or other unsuitable material for its audience

certification   giving limits to the age group which can watch a particular film

clapperboard   either an electronic device or a hinged board with information such as the time and date, and the take of the scene about to be shot. The board is clapped in front of the movie camera or, if automated, makes an electronic noise so that these details are recorded and the pictures and sound can later be synchronized.

close-up   camera shot made close to its subject

console   piece of equipment that stores and mixes music and sound effects

continuity   making sure that the sets, props, costumes and make-up do not change from one sequence of shots to another when they are not supposed to, even if the sequences are shot on different days

copyright   the right to control an original idea; the owner is usually the creator of that material

cutting   when the director orders the camera operator to stop shooting a sequence; or the way in which a film is putting together in the editing stage

diffused   scattered out over a wide area

digital   using computer technology

digital manipulation   rearranging shots or parts of shots on a computer screen by moving around parts of the screened image or images

distribute   to negotiate with cinemas and other venues for the right to screen a film

edit   to cut down and rearrange recorded material

enveloping sound   film sound that is broadcast to the audience from different directions

fill light   diffused lighting (see above) used on set to fade unwanted shadows

filter   transparent coloured discs fitted on to a camera lens to filter light and alter the final colour of a projected scene

final print   finished master film from which all copies are made, ready for distribution

genre   type or category of film, such as action movie, comedy, costume drama and so on

hydraulic brace   flexible arm used to fix a camera on to a special vest worn by the camera operator; it allows movement without shaking the camera

investment   to plough money into a film so that it can be produced, with the expectation of receiving profits from the film when it is released

lighting plot   plan showing the positions and strengths of lamps used in each filmed sequence

morphing   the digital manipulation of images to make solid objects appear to change

musical notation   written music

optical viewfinder   'eye' through which the camera operator sees the frame which he or she is shooting

point-of-view technique   filming over the shoulder of the actor, as if the scene being filmed is what the actor is actually seeing

post-production   all the editing and recording procedures that take place after filming has been completed

pre-production   all the preparation that takes place before shooting beings, such as completing the filmscript and finding the location

preview   a viewing of the film before it is publicly released

producer   person in overall charge of the finance, control and planning of a film

prop   objects placed on a film set or location, or which the actor carries or wears

rating   kind of certificate issued for each film according to the age group that is allowed to watch it

rights   the ownership of a film, written script, recorded music and so on; the right to use or broadcast it can be sold to someone else

rushes   first prints of the day's film shooting, viewed by the director and other members of the team

screenplay   film script of an existing play, novel and so on, or an original idea

sequel   follow-up film, often using the same characters or scenario

set   specially designed and built structure, for example a building or room, in which filming takes place

short   film that is usually only about 30 minutes long, rather than a feature film, which lasts about an hour and a half

subgenre   genre (see above) that is divided further into different types; so an action movie genre is divided into action comedy, action adventure and so on

synthesized   sound that is reproduced by a machine called synthesizer rather than by real instruments or other sources

take   version of a shot or sequence; it often requires several takes to get the shot that the director wants

think-tank   group of people employed to come up with an original or good idea

unit production manager   on a large production, the person who is responsible for the scheduling and budgeting of their particular unit. The unit production manager makes sure that the film as a whole runs to time and on budget.

widescreen   cinema screen that is a lot wider than it is deep; it can be used to extend the action so that it is not just concentrated in the centre of the screen

Index